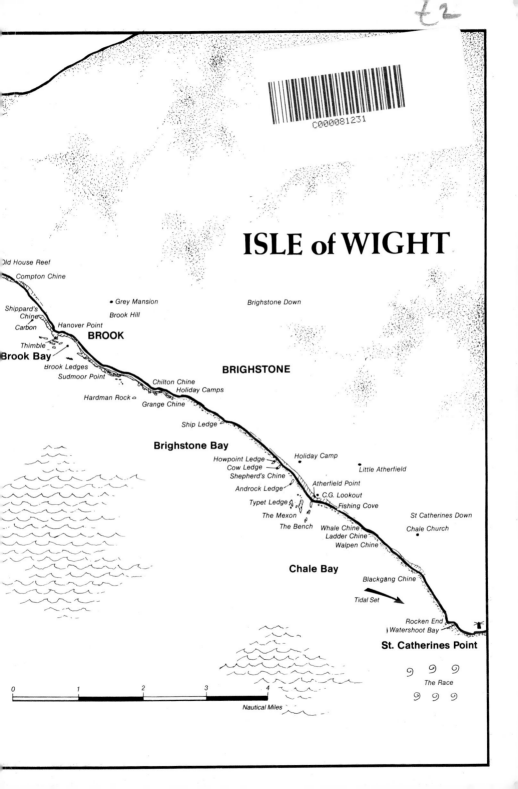

ISLE of WIGHT

Old House Reef

Compton Chine

Shippard's Chine

Carbon • Grey Mansion

Hanover Point Brook Hill

Thimble **BROOK**

Brook Bay

Brook Ledges

Sudmoor Point

Hardman Rock ○

Chilton Chine

Holiday Camps

Grange Chine

Ship Ledge

Brighstone Down

BRIGHSTONE

Brighstone Bay

Howpoint Ledge

Cow Ledge

Shepherd's Chine

Androck Ledge

Typet Ledge

The Mexon

The Bench

Holiday Camp

Little Atherfield

Atherfield Point

C.G. Lookout

Fishing Cove

St Catherines Down

Chale Church

Whale Chine

Ladder Chine

Walpen Chine

Chale Bay

Blackgang Chine

Tidal Set

Rocken End

Watershoot Bay

St. Catherines Point

The Race

0   1   2   3   4

Nautical Miles

WIGHT HAZARDS
By Peter Bruce

FIRST EDITION PUBLISHED JUNE 1987
SECOND EDITION PUBLISHED DECEMBER 1989

Boldre Marine
Kestrel Cottage, Shirley Holms, Lymington, Hampshire
England, SO41 8NH
Telephone: Lymington (0590) 683106

Contents

ACKNOWLEDGEMENT

Few would have the temerity to publish a book such as this without the help of local expertise; and I have obtained much valuable information by consulting those who live on the Island coast. I am grateful to these good people for answering my questions with typical Island patience and courtesy.

CAUTION

While every care has been taken in compiling this book, it is regretted no responsibility can be taken by the author or publisher for inaccuracies or omissions, or for any accidents or mishaps resulting from its use.

Front cover: Yachts between St Anthony Rock and Sun Corner.
Photo by Roger Lean-Vercoe.

Printed by West Island Printers Ltd, Afton Road, Freshwater, Isle of Wight, PO40 9TT. Tel: (0983) 753161.

CHAPTER 1

The South Coasts of the Isle of Wight

The southern shores of the Isle of Wight have their own special hazards and charms. The coasts are exposed to the full force of channel gales which bring bigger seas than in the Solent, overfalls, dangerous lee shores and that more subtle foe, the swell. As might be expected there can be a marked difference between the shelter offered by the coastline facing the prevailing wind and that on the eastern side.

Though there are no large scale charts for much of the coast, inlets such as Scratchell's, Woody, Luccombe and Priory bays are well worth a visit when the weather is right. The water is much clearer than in the Solent, bird life is more prolific, fishing is richer and there is seldom a crowd. In addition the Island coast is a corner of a main sea route, and having been once a centre of smuggling it has much of historical interest.

Old wrecks present a risk to vessels going near to the shore, besides several rocks and ledges which have wrought the destruction of a large number of vessels over the years, particularly in winter and before the invention of radar. At the turn of the century the exposed coast lying between the Needles and St Catherine's point, known locally as the Back of the Wight, warranted no less than three rowing lifeboats in the space of six miles: one stationed at Brook, another at Brighstone and the third at Atherfield.

To cover the hazards of the outer Island coast, an imaginary voyage will be taken from the Needles channel eastwards, round St Catherine's point to No Man's Land fort. Place names are taken from local sources, Admiralty charts nos. 394, 2045, 2219, 2050 and 2022, and the Ordnance Survey map Outdoor Leisure 29 of 2 inches to 1 mile scale, which is accurate and detailed between mean high and mean low water, and therefore a valuable navigational aid when landing.

For convenience all compass bearings are given in degrees magnetic, and a variation of 5° west is assumed.

CHAPTER 2

The Needles and Tennyson Down Cliffs

It is well known that numerous craft have been badly damaged by hitting the wreck of the *Varvassi* off the Needles. Less well known is that the remnants of wreck are on a ledge, not much deeper than the wreck, which extends westwards on the same line as the present Needles rocks towards the Bridge buoy. As it is difficult to judge distance off when rounding the Needles lighthouse, it is wise to give the wreck and the ledge a wide berth. A rule of thumb, used by open fishing boats to give a depth of 4m, is to make sure the lighthouse main light will be buried in the coastguard station before the Needles come into line. Vessels with greater height of eye will need to keep further out. The inner passage is only for the bold; nevertheless, if the swirl of Goose rock can be identified, by leaving it about ten metres to port and then heading south, the deepest water will be found: 3m at chart datum on the best line (Plate 1).

There is a third option, of course, when negotiating this point, and that is to 'thread the Needles'. Though this is quite commonly done by fishing craft, it is only advisable in shallow drafted craft

Plate 1. The Needles from overhead. The broken line shows the inshore passage between Goose Rock to the east and the wreck of the Varvassi *to the west*

WRECK

GOOSE
ROCK

under power and in calm conditions with no swell. Two Dutch East Indiamen tried to do so out of dire necessity in 1627, and both were seriously damaged in the process. The remains of one of them, the *Campen*, still lie on the south side of the middle Needle.

The best time to go through is at slack water, bearing in mind that the tide is not slack for long and can run at a tremendous rate. It is just possible at low water springs in a dinghy, and whilst there is more scope at high water, one must remember that the tidal range at the Needles is only 2m at springs and 1m at neaps, as opposed to 4m at springs and 2m at neaps at Portsmouth.

One can negotiate both gaps between the Needles (Plate 2), but only canoeists can take the gap between the Needles and the shore. It is advisable, of course, to head into any current that is running, at any rate until familiar with the best line. When the tide is flooding, the water level is visibly higher in Scratchell's bay, so going with the current is like shooting rapids into nasty overfalls and white water.

The westernmost passage, i.e. the gap between the two outer Needles, has the deepest water in the centre and has one prominent rock to be avoided north-west of the middle point. When this is just showing above the surface, at least one metre will be found elsewhere. There is another rock visible in Plates 1 and 2 just south of the western end of the middle Needle which is just about awash at low water springs.

The other passage between the middle and inner Needle is wider and more generally used. All the submerged rocks obstructing the

Plate 2. The Needles looking south, showing the best lines to 'thread the Needles'.

channel are on the north side, and the best line lies about one third of the width of the gap from the middle Needle, leaving one rock to the west and the other two to the east. The westernmost rock is the highest, and if its position is in doubt it is safest to err towards the middle of the gap. It was at the western side of this gap that the 40m high pencil of rock stood called Cleopatra's Needle, or Lot's Wife, until it collapsed spectacularly in 1764 (Plate 3). Early 17th century charts show a cluster of similar pencil-shaped chalk stacks on the north-west side of what we call the Needles, and it seems as if Cleopatra's Needle was the last of them to go. One of these old charts shows a sketch of 14 such chalk stacks as well as an additional 'tooth', shaped much like the present Needles, at the point where the remains of the *Varvassi* now lie. The white pencils of rock by all accounts were a remarkable sight, and must account for the name.

If landing at the lighthouse (and permission should be obtained from Trinity House first), one should approach from the north-west, leaving Goose rock close to starboard before turning to port to go alongside the steps. A deep water channel exists between Goose rock and the spit on which the lighthouse stands, and this makes a clean approach, but a tricky one when the tide is running.

Plate 3. *Cleopatra's Needle viewed from Scratchell's Bay, taken from a map published on 20 August 1759.*

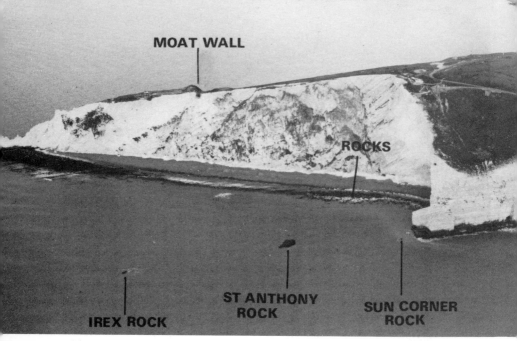

Plate 4. Scratchell's Bay looking north-east. Note that there is a submerged rock north of St Anthony, also that the rockiest part of the beach is opposite St Anthony.

Until the lighthouse is automated, the lighthouse keepers will always be glad of magazines and recent newspapers. At the time of writing full automation is planned for September 1991.

Once into Scratchell's bay (Plate 4) there are two large off-lying perils to watch for: St Anthony rock and Irex rock. Of these two, St Anthony rock, named after the treasure ship wrecked there in 1691, is the more obvious, being visible and usually surrounded by breaking water. But Irex rock, named after a full-rigged ship which was wrecked upon it on the night of 26 January 1890, is of more interest to navigators, being further offshore and only just awash at chart datum (Plate 5). It will be found by steering down the transit of the highest point of St Anthony rock and the cave behind, on a course of 087° Mag until the dry moat wall is in line on 029° Mag; but great care should be taken as solid rock rises steeply from 8m of water (Plate 6). Photographic evidence and bearings put Irex a little north-east of the inner of the two normally submerged rocks shown on the chart to the west of St Anthony, and there is only the one Irex rock to be found, rather than the two shown on the chart. Divers report that much debris from the wreck, especially iron pipes from the cargo, still lie around Irex rock.

6

Plate 5. Irex Rock looking east. Note that the highest point of St Anthony Rock is in line with the cave, known as Needles Cave, in Sun Corner; also that Old Pepper Rock is just beginning to show behind the base of the cliff.

Plate 6. Bottom contour obtained an hour before high water, showing Irex Rock when approached from seaward towards the dry moat wall in line. Soundings are in feet. A Lowrance Eagle graph recorder, as employed to hunt the Loch Ness monster, was used to obtain this trace.

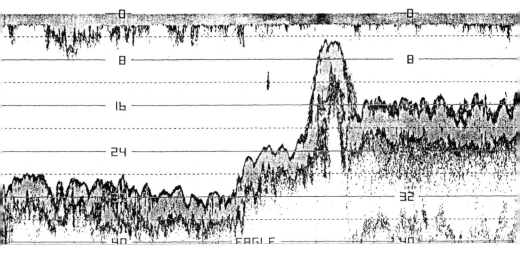

Plate 7. Scratchell's Bay beach on a calm day.

In calm weather the pebble beach at Scratchell's bay can make a delightfully secluded and sunny picnic spot, overlooked only by sea birds (Plate 7). It is best to land towards Sun Corner around high water but beware of swell. Apart from rocks along the shore opposite St Anthony rock, there is a rock off Sun Corner, awash at low water springs, with deep enough water close inside it for very small craft (Plate 8). Some major landslides took place at the cliffs in the centre of the bay early in 1988 which blocked the beach but the soft chalk soon dissolved.

Plate 8. Sun Corner Rock looking east.

Plate 9. Bench Rock.

It is worth mentioning that there is a VHF radio beacon transmitting on VHF Channel 88 from Scratchell's bay in sequence with Anvil head. It has a range of 30 miles, but it is one that needs to be referred to in the almanac as the beats have to be counted to get a bearing.

When passing Scratchell's bay one can avoid the rocks by keeping Old Pepper rock in full view when sighting down the line of the cliffs to the east of Sun Corner, known as the Main Bench. From Sun Corner on towards Old Pepper the white flinty chalk cliffs initially plunge straight into deep water. However there is a rock off the cliff some 300m west of Old Pepper which does not quite dry, and the seaweed-covered Bench rock about 200m west of Old Pepper which dries over a metre (Plate 9), besides rather a lot of other rocks within 200m of both sides of Old Pepper itself (Plate 10). One can be well clear of all of this by keeping the Needles lighthouse in view to the left of Sun Corner, though with a strong ebb tide and a westerly wind a tidal race will be felt off the point.

Plate 10. Bench Rock and Old Pepper Rock from overhead. The offshore dark line at an angle to the cliffs on the right of the picture indicates a ledge. Rocks are to be found at random inshore of this ledge.

BENCH ROCK

OLD PEPPER ROCK

9

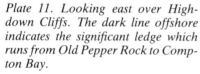

TENNYSON'S
MONUMENT

LEDGE

Plate 11. Looking east over Highdown Cliffs. The dark line offshore indicates the significant ledge which runs from Old Pepper Rock to Compton Bay.

Plate 12. Wedge rock. Numerous small offshore rocks lie between Old Pepper Rock and the caves to the east. If landing here, the cleanest approach and a small beach will be found just to the west of Wedge Rock.

Old Pepper rock (a hundred years ago it was just called Pepper rock), is the principal feature of this piece of coast. From offshore of Old Pepper a ledge runs east in a smooth curve all the way to Compton Bay (Plate 11). Passage inside this ledge is ever interesting and adventurous, as the bottom is distinctly uneven. Moreover the outlying rocks and ledges are not easily identified from seaward except by the presence of lobster pots; consequently yachts are seldom seen in here and even the larger fishing boats avoid this coast. It is helpful to know that lobster pots are often laid either side of the principal rocks and in strings along the ledge.

East of Old Pepper, more rocks appear at low water springs up to 50m offshore beyond Wedge rock (Plate 12). The caves marked on the chart as Kitchen, Parlour and Cellar were so named because a gentleman called Lord Holmes surprisingly used them for the entertainment of his guests. From these caves and on past

10

RUSTY TANK

Plate 13. Tank Rock.

Frenchman's hole to Tank rock (Plate 13) the shore is relatively clean. Incidentally, intrepid explorers will find the Cellar (Plate 14) the easiest of the caves to enter, being free of rocks when approached from the west.

Plate 14. The Cellar.

Plate 15. Adder Rock.

There are several high points on the ledge that appear at low water. One such is Tank rock, so called because there is a rusty red, bullet-riddled water tank on the cliff behind. It lies between New Ditch point and Tennyson's monument. The latter bears 043° Mag from Tank rock when viewed from a distance, but from anywhere close to, the rock is hidden by the cliff face. From Tank rock Old Pepper bears 267° Mag, a fence on the top of the cliff 290° Mag, and the tank itself 339° Mag.

Past Tennyson's monument comes Adder rock, now shown again on the latest charts. This is another high point on the ledge exposed at low water (Plate 15) with no obvious transits to locate

Plate 16. The ledge showing opposite Black Rock.

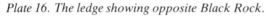

BLACK ROCK

Plate 17. Watcombe Bay looking north. Notice the ledge in the foreground.

it. Bearings to the extreme left-hand edge of Tennyson cliff on 265° Mag and Chilton chine on 117° Mag give the approximate position; moreover Black rock, a conspicuous dark stone perched on a plinth at the bottom of the cliff, is about 300m to the east of the Adder on a bearing of 072° Mag. Another drying high point on the ledge bears 198° Mag from Black rock (Plate 16).

Before getting to Freshwater bay, there is a smaller rocky inlet called Watcombe bay (Plate 17). It is dominated by two lumps of rock towards the west end, and though only worth a visit at high water it has the attraction of being inaccessible from landward. The well-covered wreck to the south of Watcombe was the *War Knight*, which was sunk by gunfire in 1918 after being mined. Though well broken up she is a popular diving site.

CHAPTER 3

Freshwater Bay

Freshwater bay (Plate 18), sometimes locally called Freshwater gate, is the marine centre, such as it is, of the south-west Island coast, and the base for an inshore rescue craft, though with little protection from the south it is by no means a safe harbour, nor always a safe beach for swimming. In summertime six or eight fishing craft lie at moorings opposite the Albion hotel on the most sheltered west side of the harbour, but before the onset of bad weather they have to be either hauled up the beach or be taken round to Yarmouth. As recently as 1988 several boats capsized at their moorings in unforeseen gales, and one broke up on the beach.

The bay is shallow at low water and rocky on both sides of the entrance, which is a gap in the chalk ledge enlarged with explosives to allow the full rigged ship *Carl,* driven ashore in a gale in 1916, to escape. The best route to enter is on a bearing of 011° Mag to a garden wall in line (Plate 19); and though visiting craft are made welcome, the shingle bottom is not good holding ground and one should not try to get in if there is an onshore wind of more than

Plate 18. Freshwater Bay looking north.

Plate 19. Freshwater Bay showing the best line of approach.

force 4, or any swell. If forced to land in unfavourable conditions, the best place is on the beach as far to the west of the moorings as possible. Incidentally, a large Union flag, 3m in the fly, is hoisted over the Redoubt fort on the west entrance of the bay between 11 a.m. and 6 p.m. in summer, giving a good indication of the local wind.

Stag, Arch and Mermaid rocks lie on a shelf of rocks on the east of the inlet (Plate 20). There is a ledge of isolated rocks further on to the east; these are awash at chart datum, but none now dry quite as much as 0.9m, which the chart suggests. A clearing bearing is 311° Mag on the left-hand edge of Stag rock, this being in line with two windows vertically disposed on the gable end of a house inshore at Freshwater. The beach behind the offshore rocks is called Butter bay. It is not easily accessible from the cliff top, but makes an interesting landing place in placid weather. As with Watcombe bay it is much easier to land at high water when the rocks are covered.

Plate 20. Stag, Arch and Mermaid Rocks. Arch Rock's name is self evident, and Mermaid is probably wishful thinking; however, Stag Rock got its name from the story that a stag once leapt onto it to evade its pursuers. Judging by the distance from the cliff, and even allowing generously for erosion, this must have happened some time ago.

15

CHAPTER 4

Compton Bay, Brook and Atherfield ledges

Compton bay is a shallow, rather desolate sandy bight. Old House reef lies along the north shore under what used to be called Afton cliff, ending at Compton corner, the point where white and brown cliffs merge (Plate 21). There are dangerous ledges at the south end of the bay that extend well out to sea from Brook point, or Hanover point as it is also called (Plate 22). At the extreme north

Plate 21. The north-east corner of Compton Bay showing Old House Reef.

Plate 22. Brook (or Hanover) Point looking north-east.

of Brook ledges, on a bearing of 319° Mag from the cairn on the ledge off Brook point, is the uncharted wreck of a 185 ton Admiralty steam tug C150, built in 1896, called *Carbon*. When bound for the breakers' yard in November 1947 she lost her tow off St Aldhelm's (Alban's) head and drifted ashore opposite High Grange (Plate 23). There was some doubt in the past about her name but recent research leaves no doubt of her identity.

Plate 23. The wreck of the Carbon *on Compton Ledge.*

The cairn, locally called the Thimble, was built at the turn of the 19th century to mark the limit of the arc of fire to the south for the Redoubt fort at Freshwater, and/or to provide an object for rangefinder calibration (Plate 24). Brook point, as with all this soft and exposed coastline, erodes apace, and when it was rather closer to the Thimble than now, the Navy used the cliff as a target for gunnery practice. The 32 pounder cannon was sited on the east side of Brook bay somewhere on the cliff opposite the old lifeboat house, and 32 pound cannon balls can be found in the pools between the Thimble and the shore. Rock strata run east/west off the point, so the ledges dry at low water springs in parallel lines.

Plate 24. The Thimble.

Many of the ledges from Brook point to Blackgang are highest at the seaward end, causing ships going aground to have great difficulty in getting off. There is no easy guide for keeping clear of Brook ledges, though if one has the visibility and can judge it, a line between Tennyson's monument and St Catherine's point is helpful. A less conservative clearing line is given by keeping the Needles lighthouse in full view from behind Sun Corner. Prudence is necessary when using this line as it will take a vessel over the outer ledges. Moreover, just south of Chilton chine less than 2m will be found, and rather less than this off Ship ledge. It is worth noting that the water turns brown over the reefs in anything but the calmest conditions, and whilst inshore fishermen find this change of colour a useful indication, deep-keeled yachts should treat it as an absolutely final warning.

Though this coast is notoriously unfriendly in a south-westerly blow, it is enjoyable to thread through the wilderness of rocks by dinghy in calm weather at low water. Past the rocks off the point, some of which are fossilised pine trees, and heading south-east for St Catherine's, there is the mainly rock-free inlet of Brook bay (Plate 25) from which an assortment of fishing boats operate (Plate 26). A conspicuous large building described as 'Grey Mansion' on the chart (and Brook Hill House on the OS map) serves as a useful reference point when entering Brook bay. Pick up the bearing of 058° Mag on this building when offshore of Brook ledges, then proceed cautiously into the bay until the shore features are visible, when one should 'come up the road' as the locals say, meaning come in on the line of the emergency approach road to the launching area. Once into the bay, one will be rewarded by finding a

Plate 25. Brook Bay.

Plate 26. Brook fishing fleet.

pleasant high water picnic anchorage at a point which appears on the chart to be nothing but a tangle of ledges.

Entering Brook bay at low water, one will see rocks dried out to starboard, further to seaward of the main reef. Several names exist for these rocks, amongst them being 'Sovereign' or 'Souvenir' after the Norwegian barque which was lost there in 1916; however, the established Brook name is Stag rocks with the group inshore known as the Little Stag rocks. For two miles south of Brook bay the inshore ledges are prominent, some curved but mostly running at right angles to the shore. The beach looks less rocky as one goes further east to Atherfield point, but ledges still exist though more deeply submerged. There are salient ledges off Sudmoor point (Plate 27), and off Chilton chine where the waves tumble especially

Plate 27. Ledges off Sudmoor Point.

19

Plate 28. Ledges off Chilton Chine.

steeply (Plate 28). Incidentally, the sandstones of the undercliff along this shore are of geological interest, especially as erosion keeps exposing new attractions; but if walking along the beach from Brook past Crab pool and Taylor's rocks to Chilton chine, or vice versa, one should be careful not to get cut off by the rising tide.

Hardman rock, pronounced Harman locally, drops 3.5m on its vertical leading edge, and is to be found half a mile west of the large house at Chilton chine (Plate 29). There is a useful transit formed by the TV tower at Chillerton and a point just inside the light-coloured wall to the right of the large house on 084° Mag. Thus Hardman rock can be cleared by keeping the TV tower to the right of the wall. From the rock Brook Hill house bears 357° Mag, and

Plate 29. Hardman Rock. The seaward face of this rock is vertical, and it is possible to find deep water all round it.

Plate 30. Ship Ledge.

the Thimble 311° Mag, which is in line with a whiter patch at the western end of Afton cliffs, just before the trees appear on the skyline.

Another potentially startling hazard, Ship ledge, will be found a mile south-east of Chilton chine (Plate 30). From offshore of this ledge the TV tower at Chillerton bears about 070° Mag, otherwise it has no particular shore feature to mark it, and is only shown on the chart as a shoal with 0.9m depth. The ledge can be avoided by keeping to seaward of a line through Brook and Sudmoor points on 310° Mag, by keeping a whole Needle rock in view as well as the lighthouse, or, less conservatively, by keeping the low lying Albion hotel in view at Freshwater. This applies to the smaller ledges, How point ledge, and Cow ledge further towards Atherfield. Behind these ledges lie uniform cliffs famous for fossils and slippery clay.

Atherfield ledge (Plate 31) consists of two groups of rocks which

Plate 31. Atherfield Ledges looking north-east.

TYPET LEDGE

THE BENCH

THE MEXON

21

dry out up to 400m offshore. To the west is the Mexon, a slab of rock 200m by 80m, and to the east the Bench, a narrower ledge which, well-submerged, extends some miles out into the bay. The unlit Atherfield buoy was removed for reasons of economy on 7 August 1988, but the position of the ledge can still be identified by the tide race running over the Bench which can be quite fierce at spring tides.

Atherfield was the most notorious of the Island hazards in the days of sailing ships, and on the bottom there is a confusion of plates and beams from fine craft such as the *Auguste,* the *Alcester* and the *Sirenia.* Most vessels have been lost along this coast in fog; in addition, if a square-rigged vessel failed to make enough offing at St Catherine's point in a strong onshore wind, she would have insufficient windward ability to get out of Chale bay, thus ending up on Atherfield ledge.

To the east of Atherfield there are now four chines (the local word for a ravine or cleft in the cliff) – namely Whale, Ladder, Walpen and New chines (Plate 32). To avoid going aground on Atherfield ledge when working along the shore, local fishermen keep outside a line between Ladder chine and Chale church, with its white flagstaff, which lies on a bearing of 116° Mag. Yachtsmen with deep keels will want to give the ledge a wider berth, especially if a sea is running. More generous clearance of Atherfield ledge is given by keeping outside the line of Brook point and the highest part of the white chalk of Afton cliff (to the east of Freshwater gate) on 321° Mag.

Plate 32. Chale Bay chines.

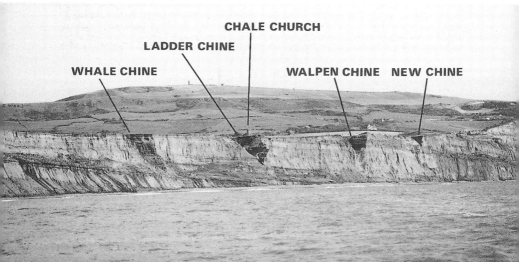

Plate 33. The fishing cove at Atherfield.

Also to the east of Atherfield point there is a cove where the lifeboat used to be launched which was, in addition, the home of a dozen or more fishing boats; but not so many are to be seen there now (Plate 33). Old maps show Atherfield point as more salient, thereby giving more protection, but the steep beach is still a surprisingly sheltered landing place, especially at low water when the ledge's screening effect is more effective. Care should be taken to avoid the numerous fish float lines just offshore.

Plate 34. Blackgang bares.

CHAPTER 5

Rocken End to St Catherine's Point

The east end of the long beach of Chale bay, with its interesting rock formations and crumbling cliff, is popular with people for whom beach clothing is optional. They are known locally as Blackgang Bares (Plate 34). The beach finishes at Rocken End where there is the distinctive Shag rock with the shape and size of an African mud hut (Plate 35). It is the start of a wild and rockbound coast where there are no easy landing places at low water until one gets to Sandown bay (Plate 36). Local divers report that the uncharted wreck of the *Wheatfield,* a steamer which went ashore in 1882, lies 200m due west of Shag rock, opposite the

Plate 35. Shag Rock with shag.

Plate 36. Watershoot Bay and St Catherine's Point looking east.

naturists' caravans. Her two large and solid boilers stand 4m above the seabed in a charted depth of about 8m of water; though probably not presenting a hazard to vessels likely to be that close in, they might well give a twinge to someone looking at an echo sounder.

Immediately to the south-east of Rocken End is an inlet called Watershoot bay (Plate 37), a pretty rock cove possibly named after a sloop lost there in 1755. It would seem rare to have the right weather to land, yet in the past fishermen and smugglers used to operate from here. Entry is very difficult, with the best approach from the north-west at high water, leaving Shark rock to starboard.

Plate 37. Watershoot Bay looking north-east. Note the darker patches to the right of the picture which are submerged rocks where Jeremy Rock used to be.

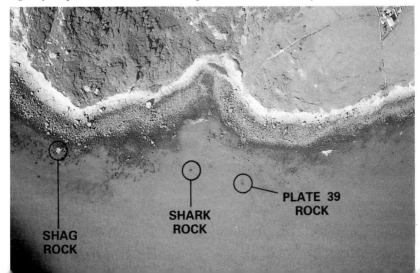

Plate 38. *Shark Rock, with Shag Rock in the background, looking north-west.*

The best bit of beach for landing is in the south-east corner. From Shark rock, which looks rather like a shark's dorsal fin (Plate 38), St Catherine's light bears 100° Mag and Shag rock 310° Mag.

Further south, off-lying rocks can be seen when St Catherine's bears 095° Mag (Plate 39) and 051° Mag (West St Cat's rock), but nothing shows above water at the point indicated on the chart as Jeremy rock. In 1752 there is a record of a sloop being cast upon 'Jersey' rock in the immediate area; a map published on 15 June 1826 shows 'Jerome' rock as an island of some 100m diameter in the present charted position of Jeremy rock, and there is an account of the London steamer *Cayo Soto* running aground just outside the Jeremy rock at 2.05 a.m. on 24 October 1908. Admiralty charts, such as that of 1852, show Jeremy rock as a drying rock one cable offshore with an outline but no drying height, whereas modern charts give it the star of a drying rock, but again no drying height.

Though some later charts show Jeremy rock in a different position, just to seaward of Shag rock, it seems as if there must have once been a substantial drying rock in the present Admiralty charted position. Aerial photographs taken at low water spring tides show several rocks not far below the surface close to the charted position of Jeremy rock; from the outermost of these St Catherine's light bears 086° Mag, Shag rock 318° Mag and the most

Plate 39. *The off-lying rock at the south end of Watershoot Bay.*

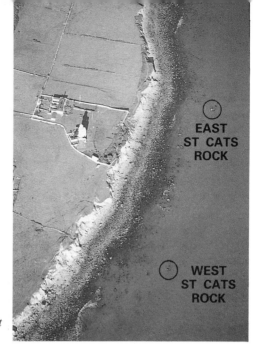

EAST ST CATS ROCK

WEST ST CATS ROCK

Plate 40. St Catherine's Point from overhead.

left-hand of the radio aerials at Niton 035° Mag. This sticks up nearly 2m above the surrounding ledge, and seems most likely to be what is left of the Jeremy, which, like much of the local rock, may have been quite soft. In any case a ledge of rocks reaches out westwards from the east end of Watershoot bay, encountered more than once by Round the Island racers, and it is significant that the local fishermen tend to keep offshore between Shag rock and the lighthouse. Regrettably no satisfactory clearing transit appears to exist.

To the east of the lighthouse a large rock, called East St Cats rock, can be found two cables out when St Catherine's bears 327° Mag and the right-hand edge of Binnel point 082° Mag (Plates 40 and 41).

Plate 41. The light bears 327° Mag from East St Cats Rock.

27

CHAPTER 6

Tides between Blackgang Chine and Luccombe Bay

St Catherine's point is well known for its tide race, which is enhanced by the bow-shaped underwater ledge south of St Catherine's deep. The race not only looks dramatic but is also dangerous, especially on a flood tide. For example, the well found 24m sailing barge *Firefly* was lost there with her crew in 1906. One can avoid the worst of the race by working along the shore, but one should be prepared for nasty overfalls off Rocken End from which there may be no escape.

Another remarkably violent tide race occurs off Bordwood ledge (or Button ledge) on the south side of Luccombe. It extends nearly a mile out into Sandown bay towards the deep patch, known for some reason as Bob's hole, and is to be avoided in a south-easterly when the main channel stream is on the ebb, unless an encounter with whirlpools and boiling sea is welcomed.

As one might expect when the channel stream is west going, a strong south-east going eddy forms under Blackgang chine. Indeed, close into the beach the tidal stream always runs south-east, except for an hour or so after high water. Grim corroboration of this fact is provided by the old name for Reeth bay, which used to be Wraith bay, because so many bodies of seafarers wrecked on the west coast in the old days were carried round St Catherine's point by the current, ending up in this tidal backwater. Much the same tidal effect occurs at Luccombe bay where the tide flows south virtually all the time.

Betwixt St Catherine's point and Steephill cove, the tide inshore continues to flow east until an hour before high water; between Steephill cove and Wheeler's bay, to the east of Ventnor, the tide inshore turns easterly after three hours of channel ebb. Thus, making to the east from St Catherine's point against the main channel ebb tide, it will pay to hug the shore to take advantage of the slacker stream, which may turn favourable past Steephill. However, there are times when the high cliffs steal the wind, and in spite of the strong contrary tide, sailing yachts do better offshore.

From St Catherine's point to Dunnose there are plenty of lobster floats to give tidal guidance, but due to the strength of the flow which tends to pull them under, they have been given particularly long float lines. Thus one should be alert both to being fouled by submerged lines and to lines well uptide of their buoy. To avoid unnecessary trouble the local fishermen pulled their pots close inshore for the 1989 Round the Island race.

Plate 42. The coast looking east from Binnel Bay to Ventnor.

CHAPTER 7

St Catherine's Point to Dunnose

Seafarers usually keep a comfortable distance clear of the coast between St Catherine's point and Dunnose (Plate 42), and with good reason when there is a sea running onto a lee shore. Charts of the area are not so much inaccurate as just lacking in detail. The principal off-lying rocks are shown in the photographs but, even so, one should not push one's luck along this stretch of Island shore. Nevertheless, when the wind is very light, tidal considerations can persuade racing yachts to take risks, especially as speed over the bottom may not be enough to cause serious harm when grounding. In such circumstances a sharp bow lookout can often spot rocks, or associated weed, in time to avoid a bump; meanwhile the rest of the crew are well advised to sit down and hold on. In very settled weather one can anchor off the coves and land by dinghy. Whilst very rocky at low water, the principal bays have launch-ways where the rocks have been cleared; moreover, they face due south and, arguably, get as much sunshine as anywhere in the country.

Once clear of St Catherine's, the next headland, between Reeth bay and Puckaster cove, is encumbered with a heavy crust of rocks not shown on the chart. The reef sticks out well to the west of the point (Plate 43) and rocks extend from the other side of Reeth bay,

Plate 43. Reeth Bay looking north.

Plate 44. Castle Cove. The stake should be left to port when entering the bay.

giving a narrow entrance to Castle Haven, where a concrete ramp and small craft are to be seen (Plate 44). In days gone by this was a fashionable spot well supplied with bathing machines, whilst fishing boats used the east-facing slipway at Puckaster; but erosion has completely taken away the protecting headland here, nor is there much now left of the old slip.

Binnel bay lies between Puckaster and Binnel point, and one can edge in here, keeping a wary eye on the echo sounder and the lobster pots (Plate 45). If working close into Binnel bay, large dismembered chunks of masonry will be seen at the eastern end.

Plate 45. East end of Binnel Bay looking north.

Plate 46. The ruined harbour wall in Binnel Bay.

These are remains of an attempt by a German industrialist, Herr Spindler, to build harbour walls back in Victorian times. The walls were substantial but their foundations were on blue slipper clay, so perhaps not very surprisingly they did not survive many gales. Little is now left of this ambitious project, known as Spindler's folly (Plate 46). It should be said that he also planted hundreds of trees at Binnel bay, and they remain as a welcome addition to the attractiveness of the area.

At Binnel point allowance should be given for a 200m shelf of rocks stretching seawards, which tend to diminish in number towards Woody point and beyond, though disconcerting out-lyers exist off Sugar Loaf (Plate 47), the next promontory to the west of

Plate 47. Sugar Loaf looking north.

Plate 48. Woody Bay and Woody Point looking north.

Woody point, and still more off Woody point itself (Plate 48). After Binnel bay comes Woody bay which, though pretty, is not exactly very woody; possibly this can be explained by the fact that the old name was Hoody bay (Plate 49). There is access to the pebble beach from land by wooden steps.

Plate 49. Woody Bay.

Plate 50. Sir Richard's Cove.

To the east round Woody point, or Dody point as it also once was, will be found the inviting but inaccessible Sir Richard's cove, which has a small pebble beach (Plate 50). The approach is particularly rocky, so it is quite an achievement to be able to land here even at high water. The name came from Sir Richard Worsley who lived at Appuldurcombe house. Frustrated by his inability to assist in a naval action that he had witnessed off the coast, he was consoled by King George III with a present of captured French cannon, with which he made a gun battery on the headland between the cove named after him and the adjoining Pelham cove (Plate 51). This is the home of a single fishing boat which is launched off a slipway structure, and if landing at half tide one can

Plate 51. Pelham Cove, left, and Orchard (or St Lawrence) Cove, right.

Plate 52. Pelham Cove.

best come in on the line of the slipway as it has been cleared of rocks (Plate 52). It has a pleasant beach with access by path, besides a bit of sand, though sand along this shore does tend to come and go.

Just to the east there is another sandy inlet, known locally as Orchard bay, but named as St Lawrence cove on old charts. On the site of the present shoreside house there used to be a home built for the local excise officer in the hopes of discouraging smuggling from at least one of the Undercliff beaches. In spite of this effort, folklore suggests that the practice continued to flourish with little inconvenience.

At Steephill cove the entrance through the off-lying plateau of rocks faces west like an open mouth (Plate 53); it is an attractive

Plate 53. Steephill Cove looking north.

35

Plate 54. Steephill at sea level.

little bay and the home of local fishing craft which operate from the beach (Plate 54). The post at the entrance stands in the middle of the inner rocks, so it needs to be left well clear.

Ventnor is a pleasant seaside resort, and its clean sandy beach looks attractive from seaward, as indeed it is. But if anchoring in the bay, beware the off-lying rocks at less than half tide (Plate 55). It should be said that these present no real problem in calm weather, provided one is careful. Once ashore, one can be certain of a warm welcome. There is a narrow man-made passage through the rocks opposite the amusement arcade and another opposite the beach steps.

Plate 55. Ventnor Beach looking north.

BEAN ROCK

Plate 56. Bean Rock showing to the east of Ventnor Pier.

Plate 58. Cat Rock.

From Ventnor pier to Dunnose an echo sounder is of less value than usual as rocks are in random disposition and emerge steeply from a flat sandy seabed. One such is Bean rock (Plate 56), not that this one is difficult to pin-point. Wheelers bay lies half a mile to the east of Ventnor pier at the point where the chart shows three drying rocks. In fact the bay consists of a large drying reef known as Ventnor rocks (Plate 57) with one dominant impediment to navigation called Cat rock (Plate 58). From Cat rock the radio mast

Plate 57. Wheeler's Bay and Ventnor Rocks.

CAT ROCK

37

BORDWOOD
LEDG

STE
BAY

MONKS
BAY

HORSESHOE BAY

Plate 59. Church Rocks.

bears 344° Mag, Ventnor pier end 265° Mag and the edge of headland 064° Mag. Further east the stubby Church rocks on a bed of
flat sand off Bonchurch are to be found (Plate 59). These rocks are
marked on the chart and are well known, but either out of
enthusiasm to get out of the tide, or over reliance on an echo
sounder, they have often brought grief to passing craft.

A general guide to avoiding these rocks is to sight the end of
Ventnor pier with Woody point behind and ensure that adequate
land is clear of the pier, taking into account that from the outermost of the rocks Ventnor pier end bears 256° Mag (Plate 60).

It is possible to ignore this bearing when approaching Dunnose
as the rocks follow the curve of the coastline, but one should stay
in deep water until well past the slipway at Monk's bay, off which
lies the last reef of big boulders. Right on the point between
Monk's bay and Steel bay is where the *Underley,* a rather beautiful
fully rigged ship, went aground on 25 September 1871 in an
unexpectedly strong south-easterly. Divers report that fragments
of the wreck can still be seen after an onshore gale has scoured
away the sand.

Plate 60. Church Rocks looking west to Ventnor Pier and Woody Point.

CHAPTER 8

Sandown Bay

When Hampshire is covered in mist and murk, it often happens that the southern end of the Island is enjoying clear skies. Sandown bay not only enjoys long hours of sunshine but is sheltered from the prevailing wind, adding to its attraction for summer visitors. Navigationally speaking, Sandown is an innocuous place, except of course in a south-easterly, when it becomes like any other lee shore. Also violent gusts can come over the top of the Island in a storm, such as capsized the sail training frigate *HMS Eurydice* in 1878.

As far as yachtsmen are concerned the old smugglers' haunt of Luccombe, within Sandown bay, is of particular interest. It is a beautiful anchorage and, with its high wooded cliffs of sandstone interspersed with clay, is in itself worth a visit (Plate 61), though one should bear in mind that the neighbouring village suffers badly from cliff erosion and landslides. To the south of Luccombe bay, Bordwood ledge comes out about 120m, and to the north Yellow ledge and Horse ledge project 200m from the shore, like a pair of devil's horns (Plate 62), their presence revealed by tidal turbulence and many lobster pot floats. Rocky patches exist close inshore at Shanklin pier and further north there is a multitude of groynes with their outer limits clearly marked with beacons.

As a result of the October 1987 severe storm, at the time of writing Shanklin pier is still without its centre part, which had, only

Plate 61. Luccombe Bay.

Plate 62. Luccombe Bay to Shanklin Pier, showing Yellow Ledge and Horse Ledge.

moments before its destruction, been vacated by two fishermen who had to run for their lives. It is understood that the pier is to be rebuilt in the same Victorian style.

The *Harry Sharman,* shown on the chart at the east end of Sandown bay, was an old tug which went aground in a storm in 1970, during the salvage of the burning tanker *Pacific Glory.* As it is very exposed to the south-west, the *Harry Sharman* is disintegrating steadily; nevertheless, there is enough of her left to spoil someone's day (Plate 63). A rough and ready guide is to consider the tug to lie due south of Yarborough monument, and to be a danger when the monument has been lost from sight behind the cliff face. From the stern of the wreck the bearing of the right-hand edge of Culver cliff is 077° Mag, and that of the Yarborough monument 358° Mag.

Plate 63. The Harry Sharman, *looking east.*

41

CHAPTER 9

Culver Cliffs and Whitecliff Bay

Whitecliff bay is a pleasant anchorage, well sheltered from westerly winds but overshadowed by a caravan site on the clifftop. Approaching from the west, Shag rock will be found exactly on the line of the Culver cliffs leading out from Sandown bay, and shows up clearly except at very high tide when it may just be covered (Plate 64).

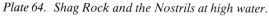

Plate 64. Shag Rock and the Nostrils at high water.

A tiny harbour in Horseshoe bay forms inshore of Shag rock at high water (Plate 65); thus in very calm conditions it is possible to go alongside the rock wall or visit the two adjoining caves looking east to Culver spit, which are known as the Nostrils. Whitecliff ledge dries out a cable from the east of Culver cliff (Plate 66), therefore one should not cut the corner when approaching White-cliff bay from Sandown. The turbulent flow over the ledge gives a clear indication of the danger when the tide is running fast.

It is interesting to note that a ridge of chalk forming the high downs runs right across the Island, connecting Culver cliffs with the white cliffs of Tennyson down. The Culver cliff chalk is soft, and cliff falls are quite common.

Plate 65. The high water harbour in Horseshoe Bay.

Plate 66. Culver Cliffs looking north.

CHAPTER 10

Bembridge Ledge

Bembridge ledge is an extensive plateau of rocks drying out three cables from the beach but sufficiently covered to cross in a small boat at high tide (Plate 67). Presence of the ledge is not at all obvious in poor visibility, and a submarine once astonished Bembridge residents by arriving there late one evening in 1968. Amongst several visitors to the ledge there was a paddle steamer called the *Empress Queen* which went aground in fog and a heavy breaking swell on 3 February 1916; in these conditions one should be especially cautious as the most prominent remains of the *Empress Queen* are not only solid, sharp and dangerous, but lie some way out from the reef (Plate 68), as was found by two British Admiral's Cup team contenders in 1985, and even local fishing boats since. Their crews are in good company as according to lifeboat diaries, Admiral David Beatty, the hero of the Battle of Jutland, was wrecked upon Bembridge ledge in a gale on 16 December 1899 when of Commander's rank, a fact not recorded by his biographers.

Plate 67. Bembridge Ledge looking west.

EMPRESS
QUEEN

WHITECLIFF BAY

LONG LEDGE

HIGH ROCKS

THE GRETON

THE RUN

FORELAND

SHARPUS ROCKS

Plate 68. Bembridge Ledge looking north-west.

From the wreck of the *Empress Queen* the left-hand edge of Culver cliff bears 241° Mag and the coastguard lookout tower bears 335° Mag. It is particularly helpful to know that the wreck is on a line with the lifeboat station, just coming into view behind Bembridge point on a bearing of about 002° Mag (Plate 69). A 1985 Admiralty Notice to Mariners gives the wreck's position as 50°40.58N, 1°04.05W, having a length of 110m, drying 1.7m and orientated on a line of 310/130°. The Queen's Harbourmaster at Portsmouth had the *Empress Queen* surveyed in 1988 with a view to disposing the wreck with explosives, but found this to be impractical.

Plate 69. Principal remains of the Empress Queen.

On Admiralty charts 2022 and 2050 the coastguard tower was once placed 200m from its true position, which was rather confusing as it is a natural choice for taking bearings. However, this has been amended by Admiralty Notices to Mariners No 1820 of September 1987, which states that 'the CG lookout station has moved to 50°50.88N 1°04.32W, ie 200m north-north-east'.

The rocks to the east of The Run, the Sharpus rocks, as the name implies, are the rampant ones of the ledge most likely to cause damage. It was here that the yacht *Barracuda of Tarrant,* famous among those who follow the television series 'Howard's Way', went ashore for real before dawn on 2 May 1988. She was coming home from the Royal Ocean Racing Club's Ouistreham race in a fresh southerly breeze on the port gybe when the Princessa shoal buoy was sighted quick flashing 9 every 15 seconds to port. This was misidentified as the Bembridge ledge buoy, which has a characteristic of 3 flashes every 10 seconds. Experienced local seafarers say that this happens quite frequently, so it is probably more easily mistaken than one would think. The author of this book was in Antigua at the time, and there is no truth in the story that he was aboard the *Barracuda*!

The passage between the Princessa shoal and the southern part of the ledge is found by lining up Culver cliff with the high land behind Ventnor. A good safe transit is on Gatcliff, the notch in the skyline at Appuldurcombe on 251° Mag; but one can take a closer course by lining up Culver cliff with the third dip in the hills to the left of Gatcliff, if one has good eyesight and good visibility. At night locals use the lights of Shanklin to avoid the ledge, most of which should be in sight to the left of Culver cliff. In daylight, when the right-hand edge of Bembridge fort is in transit with the tower of Bembridge school on 258° Mag, and Nettlestone point opens well to the right of the lifeboat house and its slipway on 328° Mag, one can head north up the channel called The Deep between Cole rock and the shore. One should be careful to avoid the mass of lobster pot floats in this area, known locally as the Minefield, and also not to get set onto the steep east side of the ledge during a spring ebb tide, which starts running two hours before high water.

Bembridge ledge is well portrayed on the large scale charts of the eastern approaches and the harbours and anchorages. These show the bulk of the ledge to the south of the point, but in addition extensive reefs turn the corner of the Foreland, requiring the lifeboat station to be positioned well out from the shore. Less obvious are the Dicky Dawe and Cole rocks, three cables offshore and on a transit between St Helen's fort and Nettlestone point. It is a rare thing to see Cole rock dry, but not so rare to see some craft aground there (Plate 70). Dicky Dawe, by the way, was a celebrated smuggler who used to sink incoming contraband kegs on these rocks, now named after him, until he judged it safe to bring them ashore.

Over a mile out to sea, to the east of the lifeboat house, a wreck with only a 3m depth is shown on the chart. This is the remains of the destroyer *HMS Velox,* mined in 1915. The most prominent parts of the ship, such as her propellor shafts, have been salvaged, and the rest of the wreck has settled into the mud, leaving little above the seabed. Therefore it would appear that she is not a danger to small craft, especially as ferries seem to pass merrily over the top. It is worth recording that the nearby Nab rock, depth 5.8m, amounts to a ridge rather than a distinct feature.

Plate 70. The eastern end of Bembridge Ledge, showing Cole Rock in the foreground.

COLE ROCK

CHAPTER 11

Bembridge Bay

Once past the line of the lifeboat pier the danger of Cole rock is over, but the Ethel and Tyne ledges continue parallel with the shore towards Node's point (Plate 71). Half a mile to the west of the lifeboat station there is a landing place of variable convenience, depending on the tide, called the Colonel's hard, opposite the Bembridge Sailing Club's race officer's hut, disused since being struck by a tree in the October 1987 storm. Long ago pleasure craft used to land their passengers here and old charts show the Colonel's hard as a pier, but now it is just a slice through the ledge and fragmented bits of hard. Garland rocks emerge up to 1m from the sand south-west of St Helen's fort, and the 0.2m diameter sewer pipe off St Helen's church shows about 0.5m above the surrounding level.

It is possible to approach St Helen's fort quite closely at high water but it is said that a shingle bank does form from time to time to seaward of it.

Priory bay, to the north of Node's point, is a quiet, pretty woodland high water anchorage. The bay dries out at low water, so it is not wise to stay long on a falling tide; and if approaching from the north one should bear in mind the rocks off Horestone, which stick out about 150m.

Plate 71. St Helen's Fort looking south-east to Bembridge Point.

THE COLONELS HARD

GARLAND ROCKS

CHAPTER 12

Seaview

The shallow Seagrove bay (Plate 72) lies to the south of Seaview. The part nearest Horestone point can make a pleasant high water anchorage, but it is uncomfortably rocky at the Seaview end. Here a 0.2m sewer pipe runs out from the slipway, which is nornally marked with a red conical buoy; to the north of the buoy there is a plateau of rocks with one particularly prominent one called Big Ben. In the summer, a red and green striped stick with a yellow diamond topmark is placed in a hole in this rock made for the

Plate 72. Seagrove Bay looking south-east.

PRIORY BAY

GULL BANK

HORESTONE POINT

purpose. There is another plateau of rocks to the south of the sewer buoy, but no evidence of the rock east-south-east of the buoy drying 0.9m as shown on the east Solent chart. Nearer Seaview will be found Quay rocks, shaped like a quay, opposite the first three houses on the point; and opposite the concrete slipway, The Bunch, a cluster of rocks 70m offshore, usually marked with a yellow can buoy.

It is worth pointing out that there are a large number of unlit racing marks off Bembridge and Seaview, so a good look-out is necessary at night and in poor visibility.

Seaview makes a charming port of call when the wind is from any point in the west (Plate 73). It is only a short dinghy ride and a few paces to the centre of the village; but one should take care not to anchor off the Seaview Yacht Club slipway to avoid fouling telephone cables, and take care too when landing, as the large tidal range at Seaview makes for slippery steps. A wreck is shown on the chart 0.7 miles due east of Nettlestone point with a minimum depth of 1.1m. This was a 60m concrete barge lying north-east/south-west in a surrounding depth of 3m, but though no encounters with it have been related, the wreck was still there when surveyed by divers in 1982.

When going from Seaview to the Solent, the short cut between No Man's Land fort and the Island shore is an attractive option, and is always worth considering at high water. One should start by

Plate 73. Seaview looking south-west.

BIG BEN

QUAY ROCKS

YACHT CLUB
SLIPWAY

Plate 74. The Debnigo with Spring Vale sewer pipe behind.

getting well offshore as it quickly becomes shallow to the north of Nettlestone point at a bank known locally as the Debnigo, which extends from Puckpool point towards the fort (Plate 74). There are also 0.3m sewer pipes exposed above sand level north of Nettlestone point and at Spring Vale. The barrier to the south of No Man's Land fort, though shown on the chart, has been removed; but odd fragments of metal which are proud of the seabed may still exist. A partial survey in 1978 found obstructions with least depths of 0.9m and 1.6m. Certainly nothing shows above sea level at extreme low water springs nor have divers noticed any impediment.

NOTES

NOTES

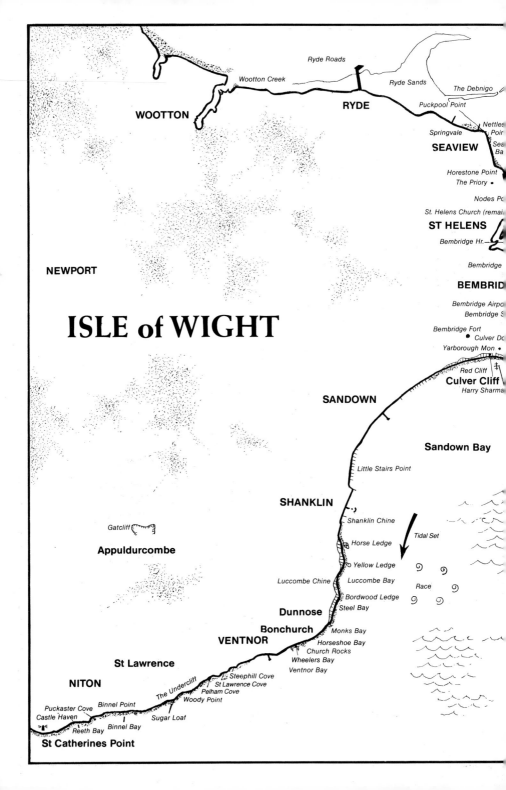